ANGELS
AND
CHRISTMAS

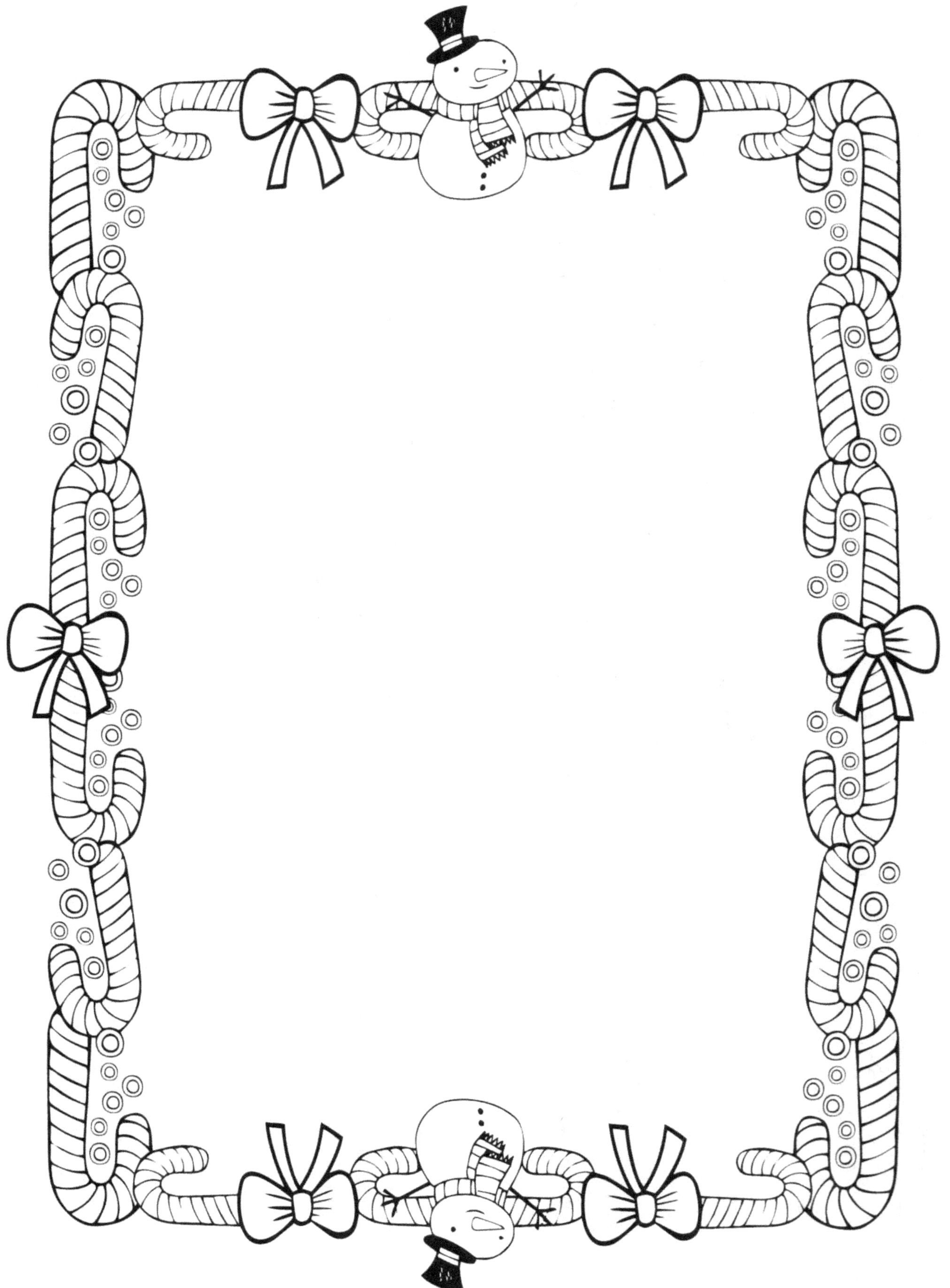

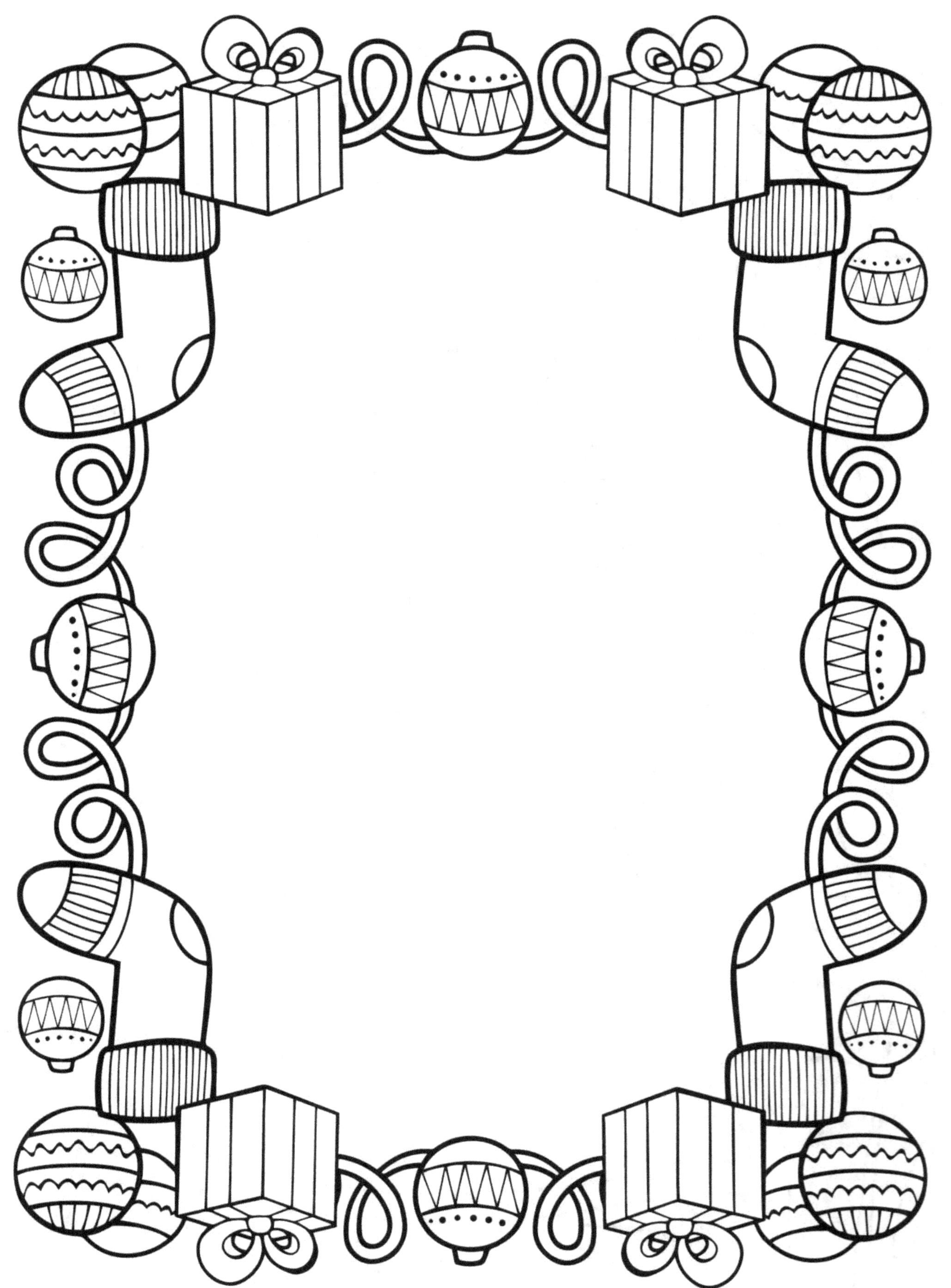

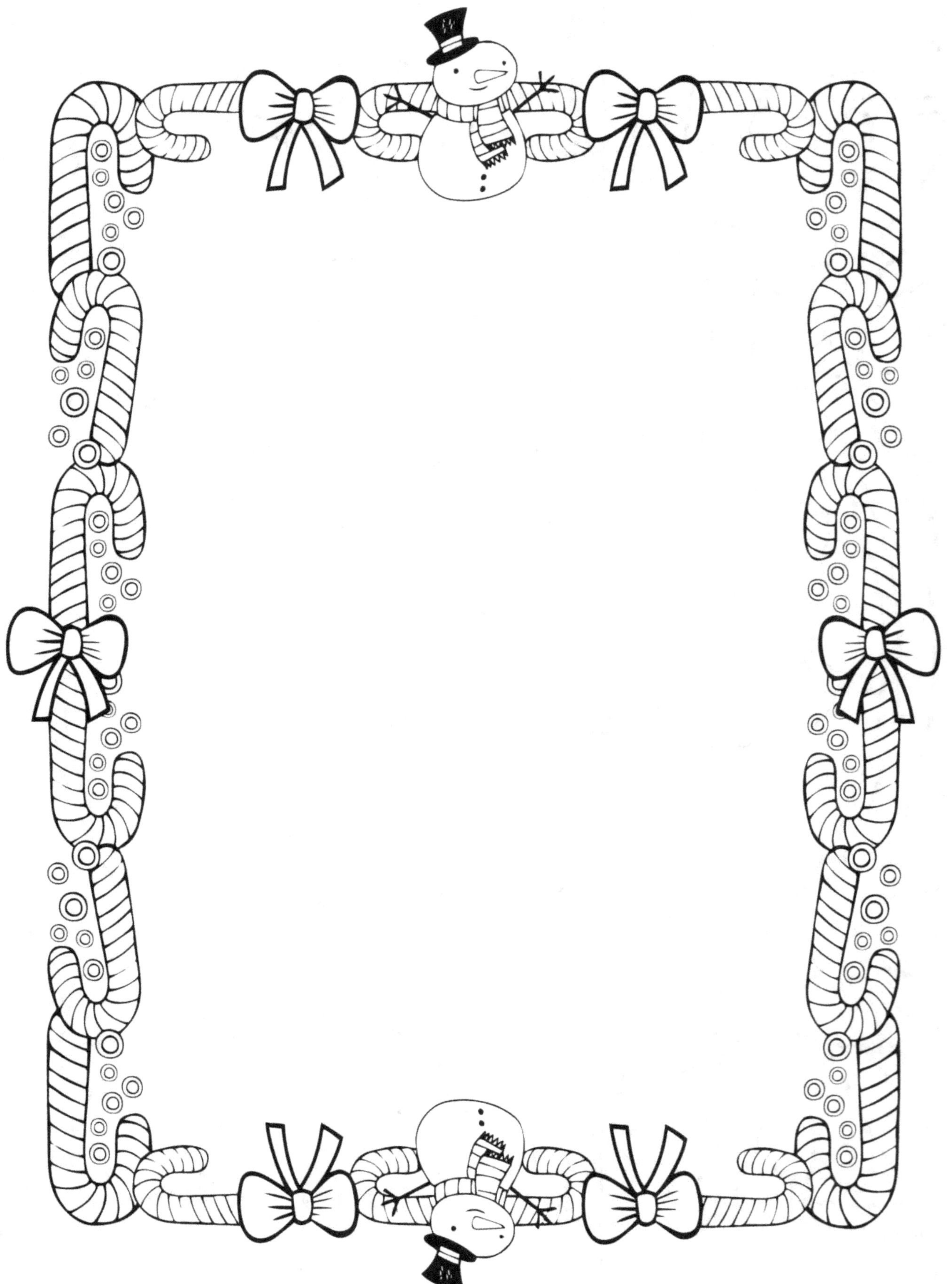

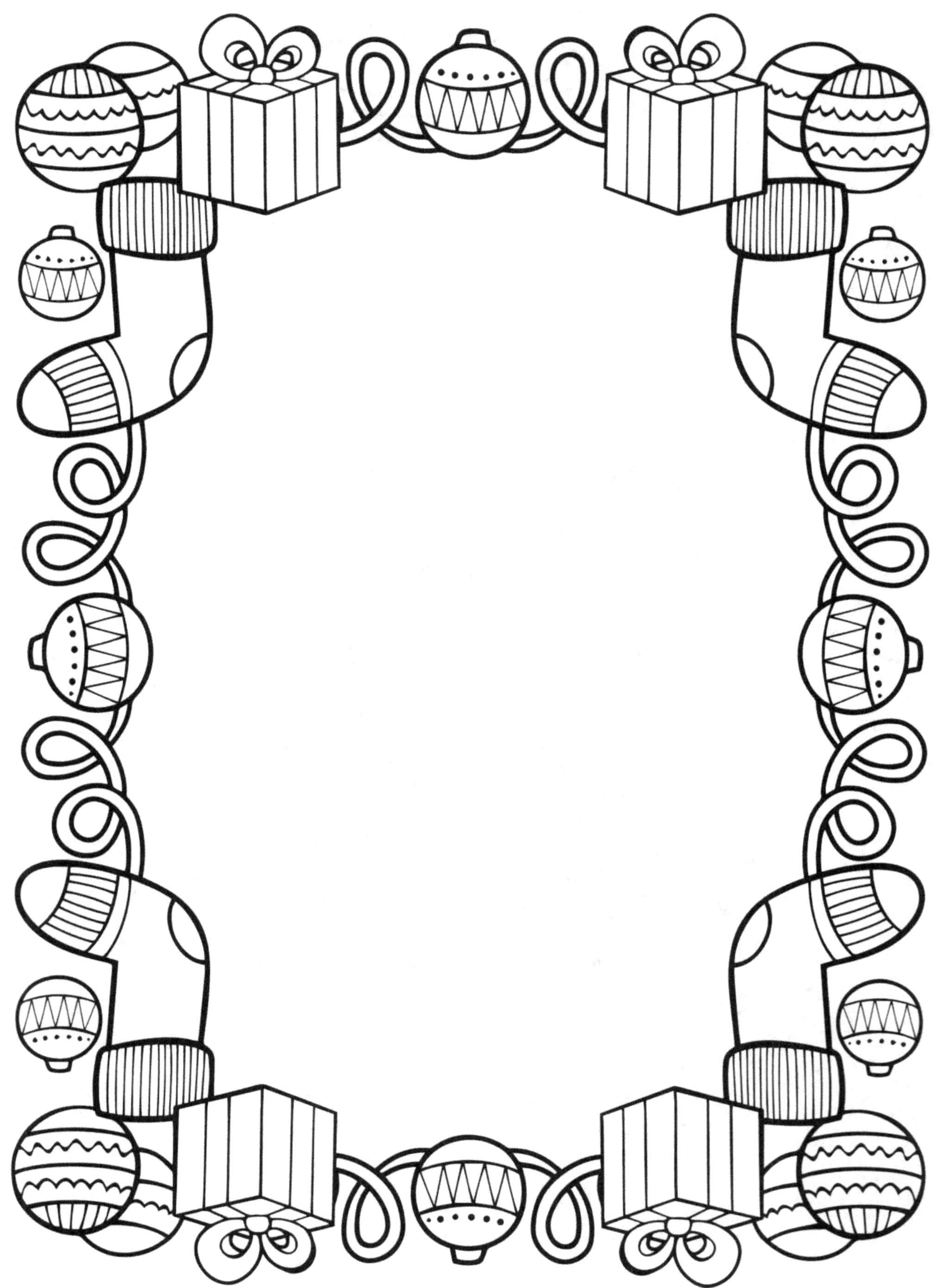

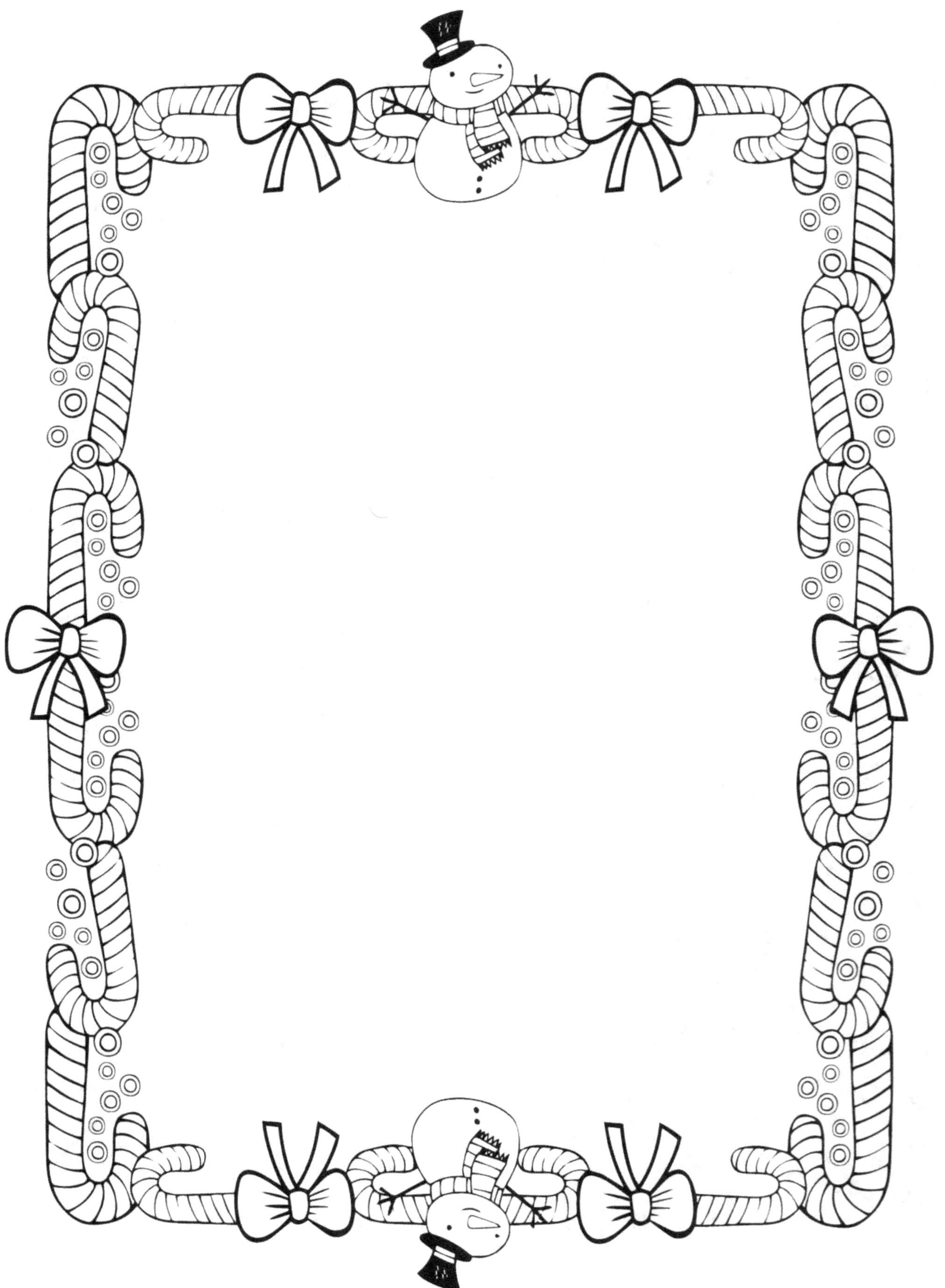

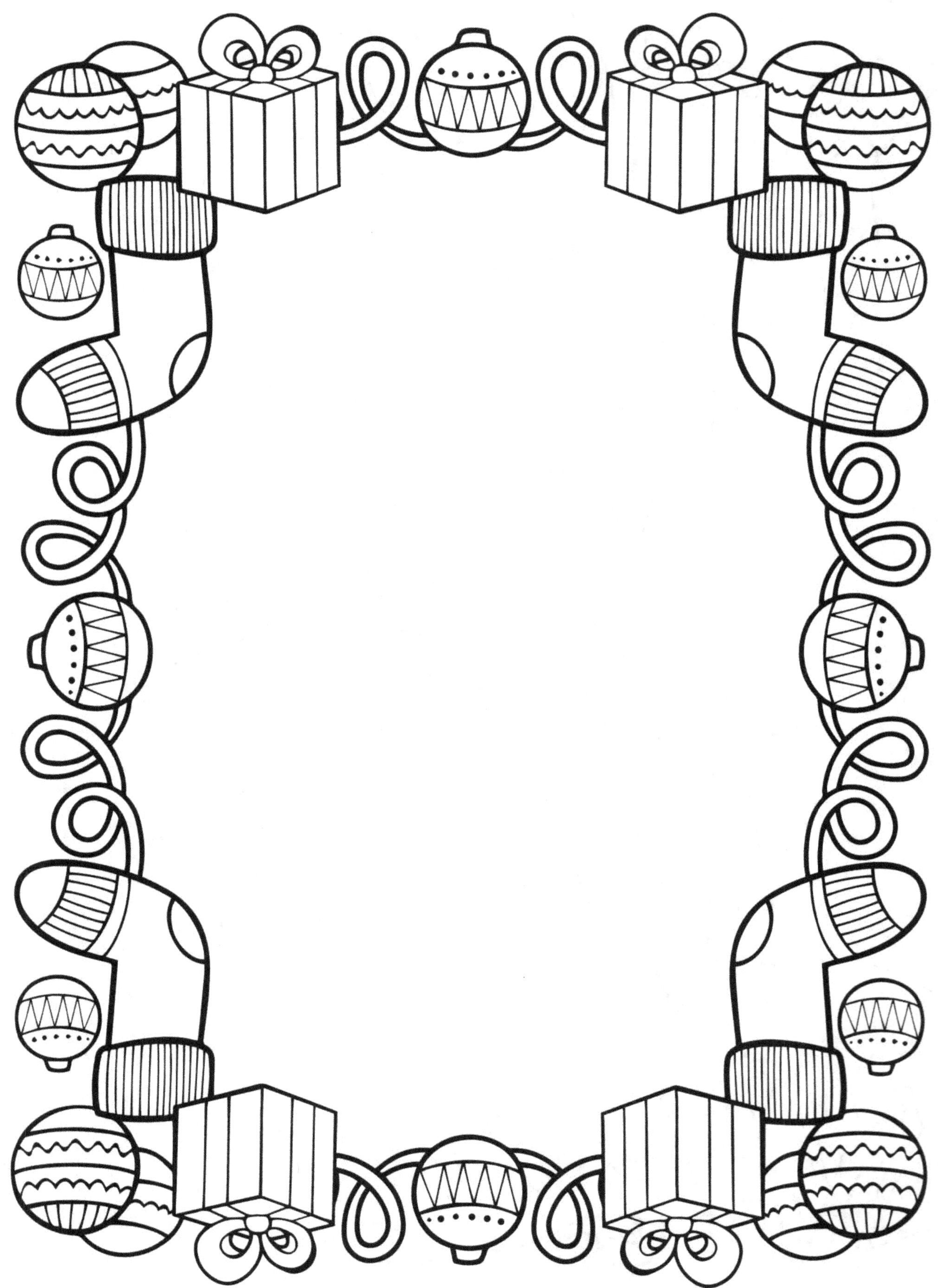

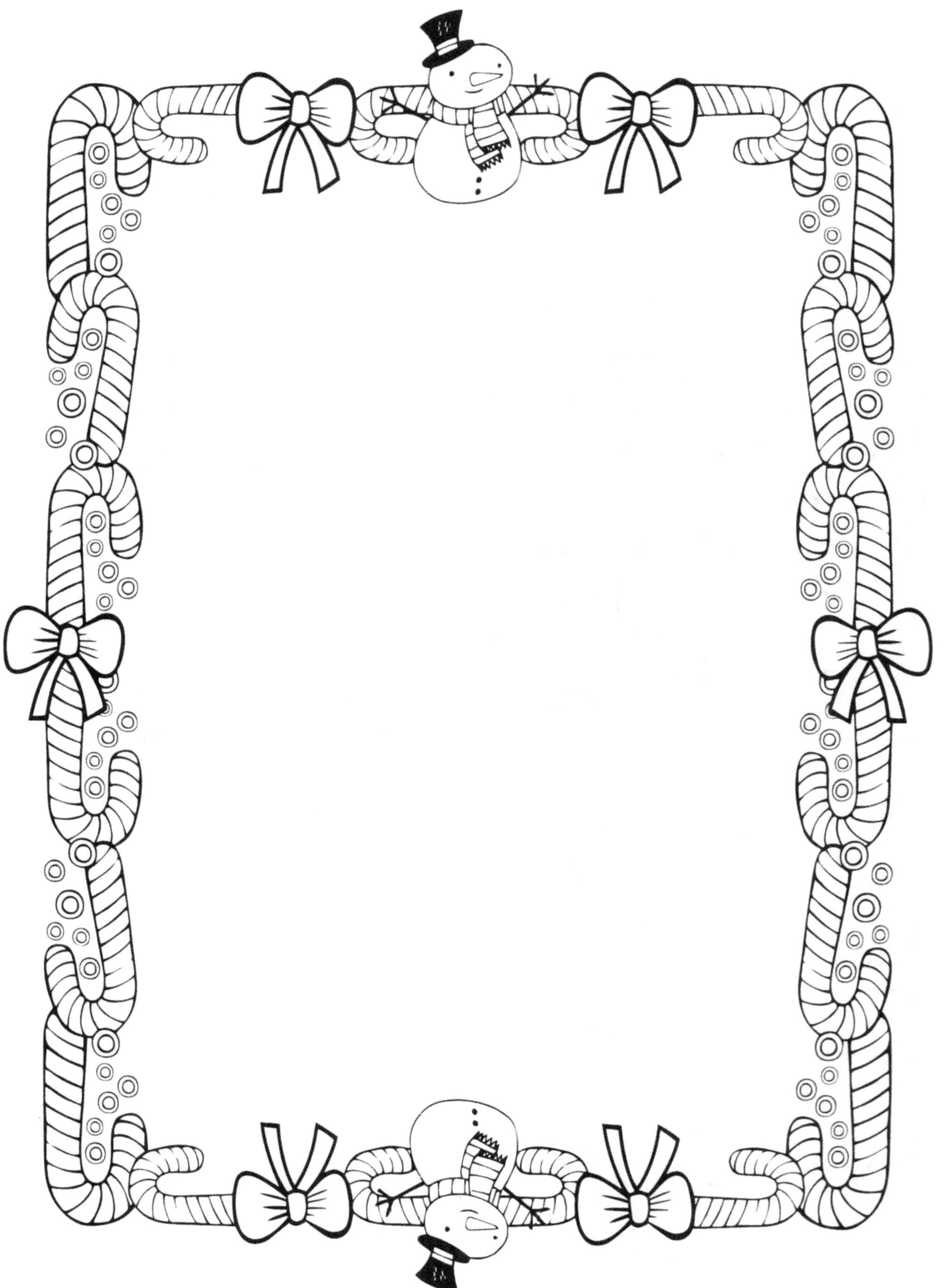

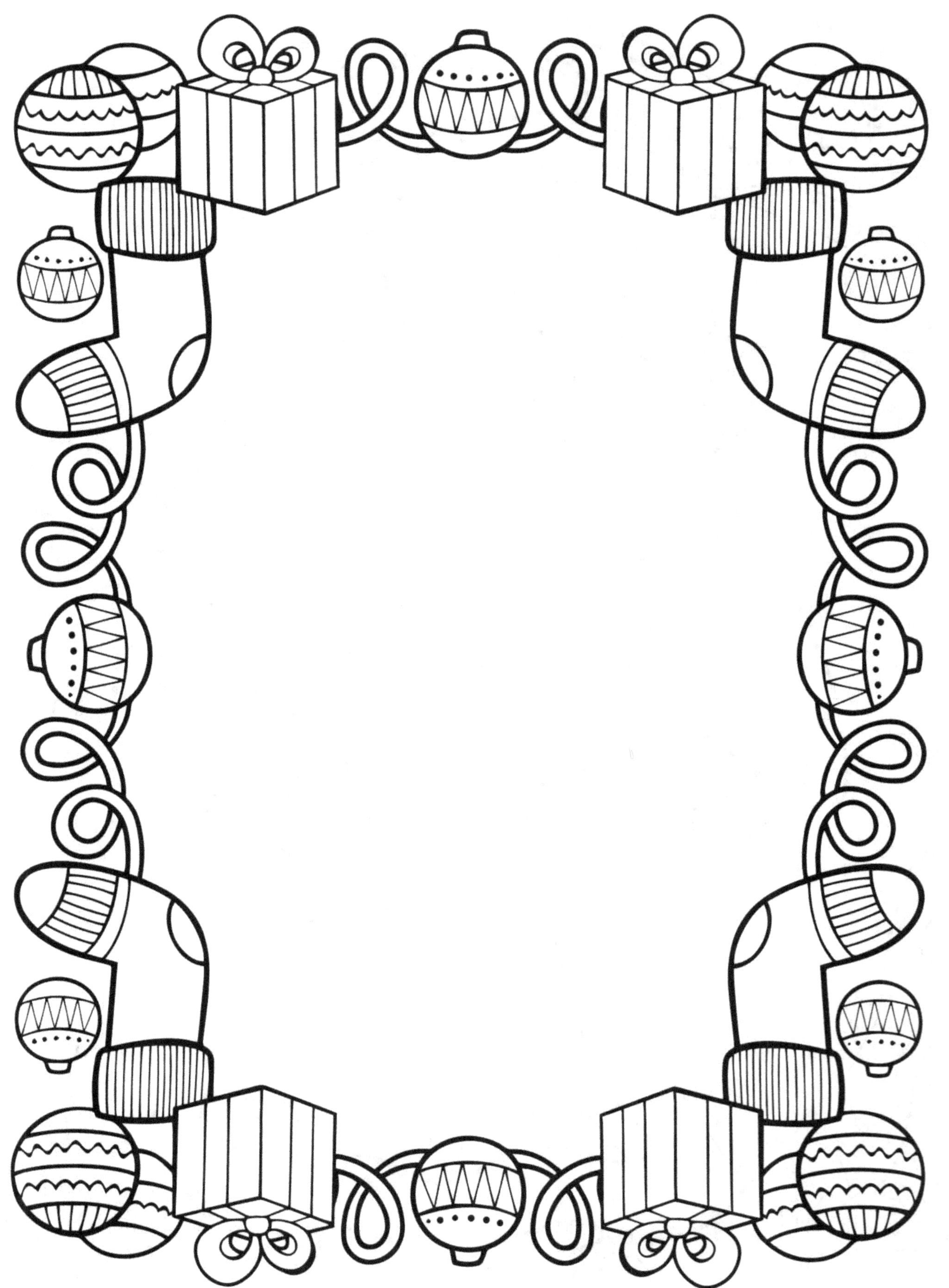

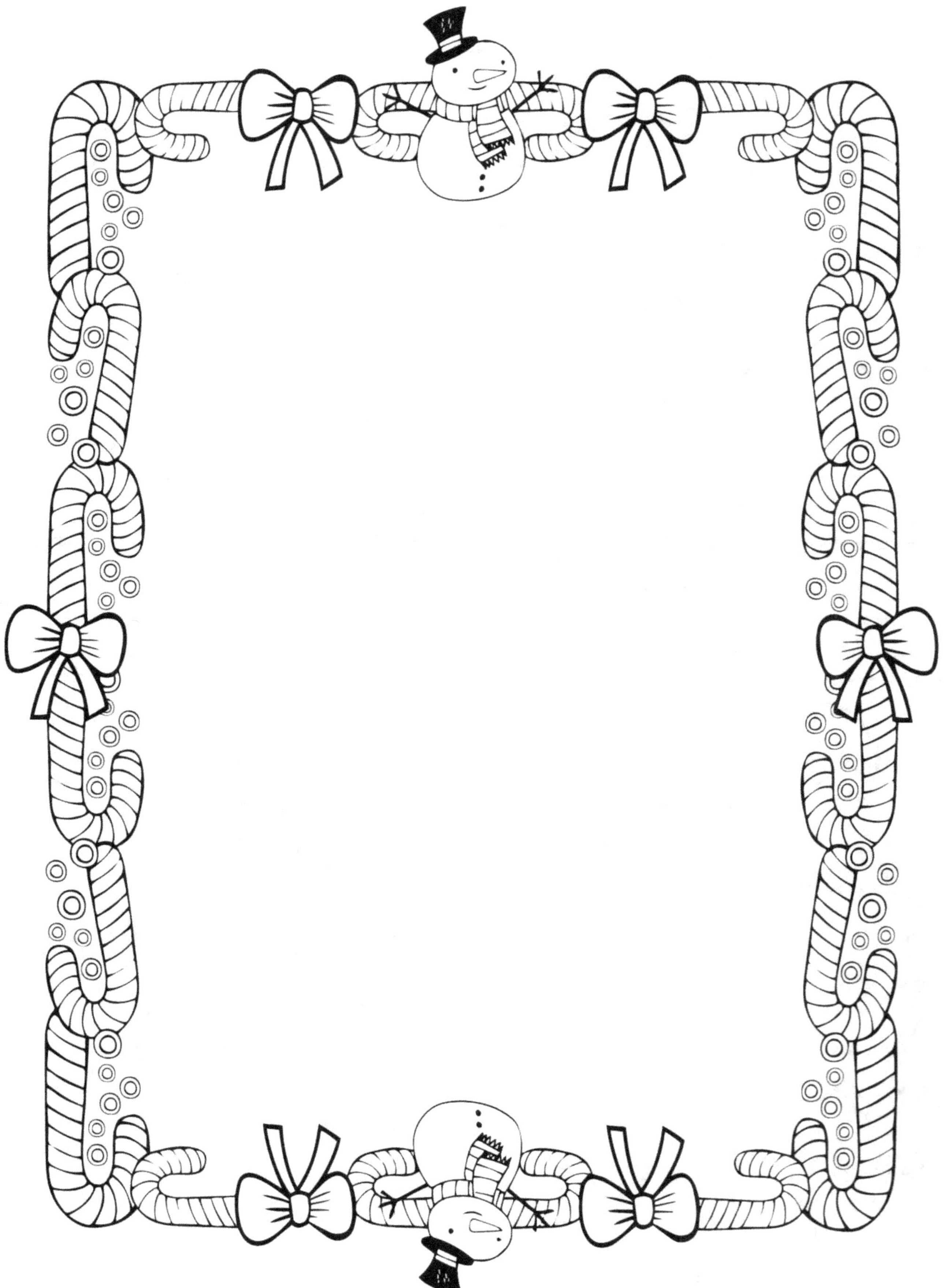

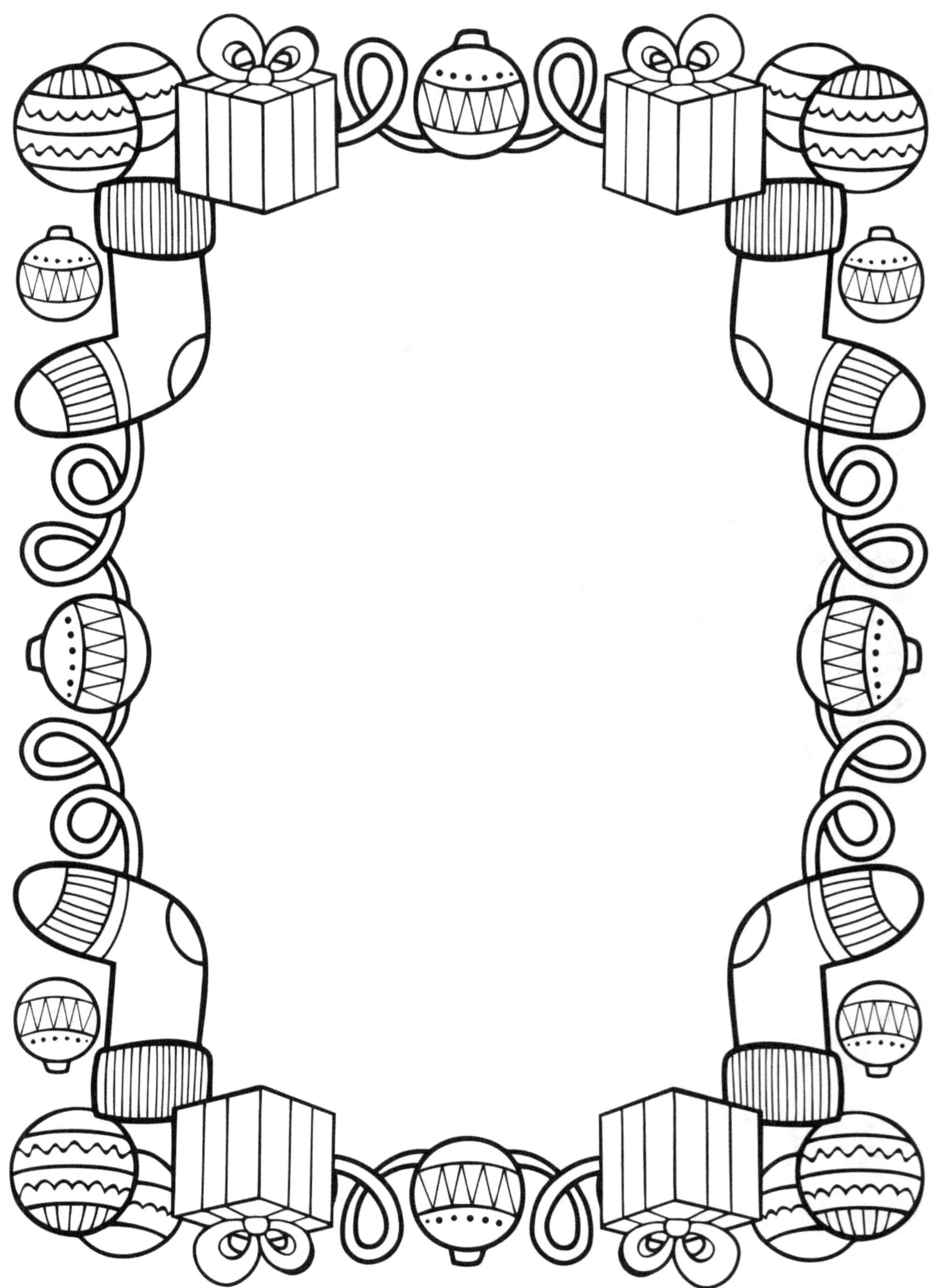

Thank you for buying my book!
I love designing them, and I am glad if they bring some joy into your life.

You might also like:

Christmas
Coloring
Challenge

ANNA
WODEHOUSE
PUBLISHING